This Cookbook Belongs To

_____

Table Of Contents

Table Of Contents

Recipe Name _____

Ingredients

_____

_____

_____

_____

_____

_____

_____

_____

_____

_____

_____

_____

_____

Directions

_____

_____

_____

_____

_____

_____

_____

_____

_____

_____

Notes

_____

_____

_____

Recipe Name _____

Ingredients

_____

_____

_____

_____

_____

_____

_____

_____

_____

_____

_____

_____

Directions

_____

_____

_____

_____

_____

_____

_____

_____

_____

_____

Notes

_____

_____

_____

Recipe Name _____

Ingredients

_____

_____

_____

_____

_____

_____

_____

_____

_____

_____

_____

Directions

_____

_____

_____

_____

_____

_____

_____

_____

_____

Notes

_____

_____

_____

Recipe Name _____

Ingredients

_____

_____

_____

_____

_____

_____

_____

_____

_____

_____

_____

_____

_____

Directions

_____

_____

_____

_____

_____

_____

_____

_____

_____

_____

Notes

_____

_____

_____

Recipe Name _____

Ingredients

_____

_____

_____

_____

_____

_____

_____

_____

_____

_____

_____

_____

Directions

Notes

Recipe Name _____

Ingredients

_____

_____

_____

_____

_____

_____

_____

_____

_____

_____

_____

_____

Directions

_____

_____

_____

_____

_____

_____

_____

_____

_____

_____

Notes

_____

_____

Recipe Name _____

Ingredients

_____

_____

_____

_____

_____

_____

_____

_____

_____

_____

_____

_____

_____

Directions

Notes

Recipe Name _____

Ingredients

_____

_____

_____

_____

_____

_____

_____

_____

_____

_____

_____

_____

Directions

_____
_____
_____
_____
_____
_____
_____
_____
_____
_____

Notes

_____
_____
_____

Recipe Name _____

Ingredients

_____

_____

_____

_____

_____

_____

_____

_____

_____

_____

_____

_____

Directions

Notes

Recipe Name _____

Ingredients

_____

_____

_____

_____

_____

_____

_____

_____

_____

_____

_____

_____

Directions

Notes

Recipe Name _____

Ingredients

_____

_____

_____

_____

_____

_____

_____

_____

_____

_____

_____

_____

Directions

_____

_____

_____

_____

_____

_____

_____

_____

_____

_____

Notes

_____

_____

_____

Recipe Name _____

Ingredients

_____

_____

_____

_____

_____

_____

_____

_____

_____

_____

_____

_____

Directions

_____
_____
_____
_____
_____
_____
_____
_____
_____
_____

Notes

_____
_____
_____

Recipe Name _____

Ingredients

_____

_____

_____

_____

_____

_____

_____

_____

_____

_____

_____

_____

25

Directions

_____

_____

_____

_____

_____

_____

_____

_____

_____

_____

Notes

_____

_____

_____

Recipe Name _____

Ingredients

_____

_____

_____

_____

_____

_____

_____

_____

_____

_____

_____

_____

Directions

Notes

Recipe Name _____

Ingredients

_____

_____

_____

_____

_____

_____

_____

_____

_____

_____

_____

_____

Directions

_____

_____

_____

_____

_____

_____

_____

_____

_____

Notes

_____

_____

_____

Recipe Name _____

Ingredients

_____

_____

_____

_____

_____

_____

_____

_____

_____

_____

_____

Directions

_____

_____

_____

_____

_____

_____

_____

_____

_____

Notes

_____

_____

_____

Recipe Name

Ingredients

_____

_____

_____

_____

_____

_____

_____

_____

_____

_____

_____

_____

_____

Directions

_____

_____

_____

_____

_____

_____

_____

_____

_____

_____

Notes

_____

_____

_____

Recipe Name _____

Ingredients

_____

_____

_____

_____

_____

_____

_____

_____

_____

_____

_____

_____

_____

Directions

_____

_____

_____

_____

_____

_____

_____

_____

_____

_____

Notes

_____

_____

_____

Recipe Name _____

Ingredients

_____

_____

_____

_____

_____

_____

_____

_____

_____

_____

_____

_____

Directions

_____

_____

_____

_____

_____

_____

_____

_____

_____

Notes

_____

_____

_____

Recipe Name _____

Ingredients

_____

_____

_____

_____

_____

_____

_____

_____

_____

_____

_____

_____

Directions

Notes

Recipe Name _____

Ingredients

_____

_____

_____

_____

_____

_____

_____

_____

_____

_____

_____

_____

_____

Directions

_____

_____

_____

_____

_____

_____

_____

_____

_____

_____

Notes

_____

_____

_____

Recipe Name _____

Ingredients

_____

_____

_____

_____

_____

_____

_____

_____

_____

_____

_____

_____

Directions

_____

_____

_____

_____

_____

_____

_____

_____

_____

_____

Notes

_____

_____

_____

Recipe Name _____

Ingredients

_____

_____

_____

_____

_____

_____

_____

_____

_____

_____

_____

_____

45

Directions

_____

_____

_____

_____

_____

_____

_____

_____

_____

_____

Notes

_____

_____

_____

Recipe Name _____

Ingredients

_____

_____

_____

_____

_____

_____

_____

_____

_____

_____

_____

_____

Directions

Notes

Recipe Name _____

Ingredients

_____
_____
_____
_____
_____
_____
_____
_____
_____
_____
_____
_____

Directions

Notes

Recipe Name _____

Ingredients

_____

_____

_____

_____

_____

_____

_____

_____

_____

_____

_____

_____

Directions

_____

_____

_____

_____

_____

_____

_____

_____

_____

_____

Notes

_____

_____

_____

Recipe Name _____

Ingredients

_____

_____

_____

_____

_____

_____

_____

_____

_____

_____

_____

_____

_____

Directions

_____

_____

_____

_____

_____

_____

_____

_____

_____

_____

Notes

_____

_____

_____

Recipe Name _____

Ingredients

_____

_____

_____

_____

_____

_____

_____

_____

_____

_____

_____

_____

Directions

_____

_____

_____

_____

_____

_____

_____

_____

_____

_____

Notes

_____

_____

_____

Recipe Name _____

Ingredients

_____

_____

_____

_____

_____

_____

_____

_____

_____

_____

_____

_____

Directions

_____

_____

_____

_____

_____

_____

_____

_____

_____

_____

Notes

_____

_____

_____

Recipe Name _____

Ingredients

_____

_____

_____

_____

_____

_____

_____

_____

_____

_____

_____

_____

Directions

_____

_____

_____

_____

_____

_____

_____

_____

_____

_____

Notes

_____

_____

_____

Recipe Name _____

Ingredients

_____

_____

_____

_____

_____

_____

_____

_____

_____

_____

_____

_____

Directions

_____

_____

_____

_____

_____

_____

_____

_____

_____

_____

Notes

_____

_____

_____

Recipe Name _____

Ingredients

_____
_____
_____
_____
_____
_____
_____
_____
_____
_____
_____
_____

Directions

_____

_____

_____

_____

_____

_____

_____

_____

_____

_____

_____

Notes

_____

_____

_____

Recipe Name _____

Ingredients

_____

_____

_____

_____

_____

_____

_____

_____

_____

_____

_____

_____

_____

Directions

Notes

Recipe Name _____

Ingredients

_____

_____

_____

_____

_____

_____

_____

_____

_____

_____

_____

_____

_____

_____

Directions

_____

_____

_____

_____

_____

_____

_____

_____

_____

_____

Notes

_____

_____

_____

Recipe Name _____

Ingredients

_____

_____

_____

_____

_____

_____

_____

_____

_____

_____

_____

_____

_____

Directions

_____

_____

_____

_____

_____

_____

_____

_____

_____

_____

_____

Notes

_____

_____

_____

Recipe Name _____

Ingredients

_____

_____

_____

_____

_____

_____

_____

_____

_____

_____

_____

_____

Directions

_____

_____

_____

_____

_____

_____

_____

_____

_____

_____

Notes

_____

_____

_____

Recipe Name _____

Ingredients

_____

_____

_____

_____

_____

_____

_____

_____

_____

_____

_____

_____

Directions

_____

_____

_____

_____

_____

_____

_____

_____

_____

_____

Notes

_____

_____

_____

Recipe Name _____

Ingredients

_____

_____

_____

_____

_____

_____

_____

_____

_____

_____

_____

_____

Directions

_____

_____

_____

_____

_____

_____

_____

_____

_____

_____

Notes

_____

_____

_____

Recipe Name _____

Ingredients

_____

_____

_____

_____

_____

_____

_____

_____

_____

_____

_____

_____

Directions

_____

_____

_____

_____

_____

_____

_____

_____

_____

Notes

_____

_____

_____

Recipe Name _____

Ingredients

_____

_____

_____

_____

_____

_____

_____

_____

_____

_____

_____

Directions

_____

_____

_____

_____

_____

_____

_____

_____

_____

_____

_____

Notes

_____

_____

_____

Recipe Name _____

Ingredients

_____
_____
_____
_____
_____
_____
_____
_____
_____
_____
_____
_____
_____

Directions

Notes

Recipe Name _____

Ingredients

_____

_____

_____

_____

_____

_____

_____

_____

_____

_____

_____

_____

_____

Directions

Notes

Recipe Name _____

Ingredients

_____

_____

_____

_____

_____

_____

_____

_____

_____

_____

_____

_____

_____

_____

Directions

_____

_____

_____

_____

_____

_____

_____

_____

_____

_____

Notes

_____

_____

_____

Recipe Name _____

Ingredients

_____
_____
_____
_____
_____
_____
_____
_____
_____
_____
_____
_____
_____

Directions

_____

_____

_____

_____

_____

_____

_____

_____

_____

_____

Notes

_____

_____

_____

Recipe Name

Ingredients

Directions

Notes

Recipe Name _____

Ingredients

_____

_____

_____

_____

_____

_____

_____

_____

_____

_____

_____

_____

_____

Directions

Notes

Recipe Name _____

Ingredients

_____

_____

_____

_____

_____

_____

_____

_____

_____

_____

_____

_____

Directions

_____

_____

_____

_____

_____

_____

_____

_____

_____

_____

Notes

_____

_____

_____

Recipe Name _____

Ingredients

_____

_____

_____

_____

_____

_____

_____

_____

_____

_____

_____

Directions

_____

_____

_____

_____

_____

_____

_____

_____

_____

_____

Notes

_____

_____

_____

Recipe Name _____

Ingredients

_____

_____

_____

_____

_____

_____

_____

_____

_____

_____

_____

Directions

_____

_____

_____

_____

_____

_____

_____

_____

_____

_____

Notes

_____

_____

_____

Recipe Name _____

Ingredients

_____

_____

_____

_____

_____

_____

_____

_____

_____

_____

_____

_____

_____

Directions

_____

_____

_____

_____

_____

_____

_____

_____

Notes

_____

_____

_____

Recipe Name _____

Ingredients

_____

_____

_____

_____

_____

_____

_____

_____

_____

_____

_____

Directions

_____

_____

_____

_____

_____

_____

_____

_____

_____

_____

Notes

_____

_____

_____

Made in the USA
Monee, IL
02 December 2019